NAVIGATING THROUGH "NOW WHAT?"

THE VARIOUS CAREER CROSSROADS IN OUR LIVES

KAREN KODZIK

NAVIGATING THROUGH "NOW WHAT?"

THE VARIOUS CAREER CROSSROADS IN OUR LIVES

KAREN KODZIK

ISBN 978-0-9825912-8-4

Library of Congress Catalog Number: 2011922192

Printed in the United States of America
First Printing: February 2011
15 14 13 12 11   5 4 3 2 1

Expert Publishing, Inc.
14314 Thrush Street NW,
Andover, MN 55304-3330

Andover,   1-877-755-4966
Minnesota   www.expertpublishinginc.com

NOW WHAT?

During my thirteen years of working with hundreds of people in career transition or at a career crossroads, I have heard many stories, struggles, and frustrations. Regardless of the circumstances that lead clients to my office, their stories inevitably end with the same question: "Now what?"

These individuals are standing at the edge of a decision point in their careers, momentarily paralyzed, not quite sure of which direction to go. They feel confused and alone.

The main objective of my work is to help people sort out options and create a plan to move to that next step in their careers. The objective of this book is to let you know, during those challenging and confusing times, that you are not alone. The career crossroads you encounter are shared with many other people. Whether you are just starting your career journey, are in mid-career, or facing a crossroads in your sunset years, each life stage has its share of questions, challenges, and opportunities. Rather than feel helpless in those times, there are many ways to take back control and actively manage your career path. My ultimate reward is to witness those moments when people regain a sense of control and hope in the midst of a career crossroads — to see their options and know that they will survive and even thrive.

I am honored to share this journey with you, shine a light on your path, and offer a plan to help you step forward with a greater sense of clarity and confidence.

This book is dedicated to you.

TABLE OF CONTENTS

INTRODUCTION

In the pages that follow, I'll describe in Part One the various situations in a career journey that can bring you to a career crossroads. Understanding where you have been and how you got there will offer insight and be necessary as you assess and determine which road to choose and how to find the courage to take that next step. I trust you will find comfort in the personal stories on these pages, based on a real life scenarios of people who faced their own crossroads and — most importantly — moved forward.

The second half of the book offers universal advice on how to navigate any career crossroads you may encounter throughout life. By recognizing a crossroads as part of the human experience, you will be able to approach each one and navigate it with more clarity and confidence.

PART 1

UNDERSTANDING THE CAREER JOURNEY

Our careers span decades of our lives. Given the dynamic and changeable world of work, we come upon crossroads more and more frequently—by our choice, someone else's choice, or just by circumstance.

What brings us to a crossroads in our careers can be as subtle as an internal restlessness that won't subside or this place of uncertainty can creep up on us over time or we can abruptly fall into it.

We can arrive at a career crossroads during different developmental stages of life. Young adults ponder what they should be when they grow up with a sense of excitement and antici-pation and sometimes trepidation. It can be confusing sorting through the options, hoping the first career step isn't a misstep.

In midcareer, people can experience the exhilaration of a career on the fast track or the subtle restlessness and discontentment when things don't turn out as planned.

Looking towards the sunset years, people commonly examine life and career and shift from a mindset of accumulating wealth to a desire for more purpose-driven work, building a legacy beyond just a bank account.

Beyond us growing up and growing older, we may face a crossroads when circumstances in our lives change. A new parent who decides to take time out of a career to stay at home until the child is in school will face a crossroads when contemplating re-entering the job mar-ket. A soldier who has dedicated many years to serving the country will encounter a crossroads when entering the civilian workforce.

Sometimes it's the circumstances outside our lives that bring us to a career crossroads.

On the personal side, the onset of a disease or health condition may force you to change your career path to accommodate different limitations and capabilities. On the professional side, a change in the job or work environment can subtly or dramatically force you to re-examine your career path.

While in the job, there may be a change in your actual role that makes work no longer stimulating, satisfying, fulfilling, or a best use of your strengths. Changes within companies and organizations are as dynamic as ever. Companies are bought and sold, downsized and divested. Having many different bosses during your career is commonplace. This constant change may also cause you to reassess your situation and career options.

Career crossroads are most apparent when you are in between jobs or in transition. Whether you lost your job or left your job, you are tossed into the center of multiple career choices and decisions.

So let's take a closer look at each of these potential crossroads in the career journey and see how some people have successfully navigated them.

Crossroads in Life

Life's journey can bring you to many career crossroads whether you're driving or simply going along for the ride. Life happens and your career path can get impacted by any number of things, including some planned, some unplanned, growing up, or growing older. You could find yourself grappling with which direction to choose at various points in your life whether it is in young adulthood, mid-career, or sunset years.

THE EARLY YEARS

A first and often memorable time in life is high school graduation and perhaps preparation for college entrance exams. You started to think about life as an adult. This time is memorable because there seemed to be a lot of pressure to pick the right school, the right major, or the right path. Friends, family, and guidance counselors chimed in with advice. The choices either seemed endless or limited, depending on your financial resources. This was the first time you had to do some self exploration and balance the ideas of what you wanted to do with what others were telling you to do.

 **MEET ERIN**

Fifteen years old, sitting at the kitchen table in front of a stack of marketing materials from a dozen or so colleges across the country, some known and others new to her. Though the pressure from those around her is mounting, she is well prepared for the task of choosing a college. She took full advantage of the career exploration program at her school, accompanied her dad to take-your-daughter-to-work day, did lots of volunteering to explore what she liked to do, and visited campuses during the summer. Based on these experiences, conversations with teachers, her parents and advisors, as well as doing some good research, Erin is able to choose a college that meets her needs and goals.

Three years later, Erin packs her bags and starts classes at the University of Wisconsin. She made the best decision for her life at this first career crossroads based on good exploration, planning, and research of the countless possibilities.

Unlike Erin, some people employ a passive-avoidant strategy to career planning at this stage in life. Maybe they turned a part-time job into a full-time job to pay the rent and car payment, figuring they would sort out their careers someday. Someday never comes.

 **MEET JACK**

He had always intended to go away to college but his plan never materialized. After high school, Jack moved from part-time status to full-time status at his father's company. Compared to his peers who went to college, Jack is doing well, making money, buying lots of toys. The thought of college occasionally crosses his mind, but he can't seem to find the time now that's he's married with a family.

About fifteen years after high school, Jack hits a snag. His father's company has struggled in the recession and has to close. Jack is out of work for the first time in his life, trying to compete for jobs with only a high school diploma. He's thirty-four years old.

With little to show from his job search efforts, Jack starts taking classes through the local community college. He initially feels like a fish out of water because it's been years since he was in a classroom. He takes advantage of the academic support programs at the school, which helps him gain confidence. His program ultimately leads to a paid internship that allows him to complete a two-year degree. With a degree in hand on top of his years of experience, Jack secures a supervisor's job for a commercial developer. Taking control of his career with additional education significantly improved Jack's prospects at this career crossroads.

If, however, you were the one who jumped right into college after high school, fast forward four to five years. After years of spreading your wings, testing your limits, and gaining a sense of independence, you realize that four years have just flown by and you will soon enter (or get pushed into) the real world. Now it's time to figure out what you are going to do for the rest of your life, or at least the next few years.

Again, this can either be a crossroads backed by solid planning and preparation through specifically selected coursework, projects and internships, and even graduate school, or it can be as confusing as the first year of college.

 **MEET GARY**

Gary was a smart and successful student in high school and college. He chose a liberal arts major, which he figured would give him the most versatility. As his senior year came to a close, he realized he loved learning and the experience of college but couldn't quite envision himself as a professional. With one semester left, Gary finally decided to extend his college experience and go to law school, not because he wanted to be a lawyer but only because he could continue learning.

It's now eight years later. Gary arrives at my office feeling dissatisfied and unfulfilled practicing law. When asked why he chose law school, he said school came easy to him and he didn't know what else to do.

Before assessing other career paths, Gary first had to overcome the guilt of potentially disappointing his family, since they're so proud to have a lawyer in the family. Taking a step back to assess the emotional factors of a career crossroads, in this case, is important because Gary's next move needs to switch from a passive to active and intentional approach to career planning.

Interestingly, how you approach crossroads in the early developmental years can set a pattern as to how you approach future career decisions. If you approach early crossroads by planning fully and assessing and preparing for various options, navigating future crossroads will likely be easier. If, however, you took a passive approach to career decision-making, you will likely wonder how you ended up on your current course. It's the difference between paddling down the river in a kayak vs. drifting on an inner tube. One way is purposeful and active while the other is random and passive; you end up down the river either way, but a purposeful and active experience often feels more exhilarating at the end. A random and passive experience might feel disappointing or bring anxiety.

MID-CAREER—LIFE EVENTS

In the course of your estimated forty or fifty years of work, there are other life events that put you at a career crossroads. Some are happy life events and others are more challenging.

Professional women often find themselves at a career decision point after having a baby and staying home until the child goes to school. They are re-entering the workforce after being sidelined or working part-time for six to ten years. This is often a time when women and whole families reassess career options. The career path the woman chooses may be the same path she was on before she was pregnant, a similar path, or completely different from her previous career path. She may take this time to retrain or even start a business. The biggest challenge these women face is the workforce they re-enter changed since they left.

Their skills may be rusty, and they may be out of touch with a professional network. Their biggest challenge in re-entering the workforce is convincing a prospective employer that their skills are sharp, current with the industry, and that they are still connected within the profession.

 MEET LINDSEY

B.C (before children) Lindsey made almost a half-million dollars selling technical equipment to hospitals. Lindsey and her husband decided that when they finally became pregnant, Lindsey would stay at home with the kids. Lindsey has now been out of the job market for six years. The day she registered her youngest son for kindergarten, Lindsey started the re-entry process. Though Lindsey was previously successful in her career, she harbors many doubts. She questions if she can compete in the job market. She wonders if the game has changed. She wonders if any of her colleagues will even remember her. But she moves forward despite her doubts.

The process starts with her need to clarify her career objective. She has to decide if she should return to work in the same or similar role to the one she had or if it's time for something new. Through the self-assessment process, Lindsey determines that she likes what she used to do and wants to return to that. Her first step, however, is to do some research to make sure the job she used to do still exists and determine how it has changed. She then has to re-engage her network to let them know what her plans are and to glean from them what is new in the profession. Lindsey starts reading professional journals and attending professional events so she can understand the hot issues in her field. She also has to update her resume and prepare to respond to employer inquiries about what she's been up to for the past six years. This whole process takes ten months, but Lindsey eventually returns to a similar role selling medical technology to hospitals and clinics. Her clarity of intention and action steps to re-enter her previous career field pay off at this career crossroads.

Another type of re-entry for women is after a divorce when they are forced back into the workplace or must increase their salaries. These women are often at a loss as to where to even begin considering their options. They may need additional education and skills to compete in the job market or have to find a role that can accommodate single parenthood.

 **MEET ANNA**

Anna met her husband, Mark, in college when she was studying to be an interior designer. Shortly after college, she got pregnant. She and Mark decided to raise a family with Anna being the primary caregiver. After twelve years and three children, the marriage fell apart and Mark left.

Anna has to support herself with a college degree but no experience. She is overwhelmed and has no idea where to start. She takes a career life planning class and discovers she still has a creative bent and wants to use that in some capacity. However being a single parent, she also needs a job that gives her flexibility and benefits.

Anna decides to go back to school for a two-year degree in web design. She is currently a contract web designer and works from home so she can meet her kids when they come off the school bus every day. The benefit of active career management gives Anna confidence as she fulfills a former dream and cares for her family.

Like Lindsey and Anna, soldiers returning from active duty may experience a very similar career crossroads as they re-enter the workforce after being deployed for an extended period of time. Though many can return to their old jobs, many cannot and they find themselves reassessing their options. They, too, will have to convince prospective employers that their skills are current and sharp. One enormous asset returning military personnel have is an incredible fraternal network they can leverage to identify opportunities.

 **MEET RICK**

Rick was a crewman in the Navy Reserves and was deployed twice in three years for the duration of eighteen months. His civilian job was in customer service for a trucking company, but because his employer was small, they were unable to hold his job open.

Rick's biggest challenge is to understand how the combination of his military and civilian experience translates into other civilian career options. After working with a career counselor, Rick identifies his transferable skills and clearly articulates them on his resume and during interviews. Rick learns how to translate his military experience into skills and assets for a civilian employer. After several months, he secures a dispatcher job for a fleet company. Following this career crossroads, Rick is happily employed and acclimated to civilian life again.

Retiring military also face a unique career crossroads as they assess how to transfer their skills into a civilian capacity and learn how to navigate very different work environments and cultures as well as how to communicate their previous accomplishments to a non-military audience.

 **MEET MATT**

Matt was a commissioned officer in the air force. After twenty-five years of active duty, he retired at age forty-five. Recognizing he still has things to offer, he assesses his career options in the civilian world. Matt was highly trained and successful as a leader and liked managing processes, projects, and people.

After talking to a franchise consultant, Matt takes some of his pension and buys a cleaning franchise where he can use his leadership skills to hire and develop entry-level workers to clean commercial office buildings. Matt has now expanded his franchise to a three-state area and enjoys the freedom of being his own boss.

Another mid-career crossroads can come when someone has a medical condition or illness that redefines their abilities and capabilities.

Doing the job they used to do, and possibly even trained for, may no longer be an option. Not only do these people need to look forward to new possibilities, they also need to let go of what they used to do in order to create a whole new identity.

 MEET STEVE

He was an airline pilot diagnosed with adult onset seizure disorder. Flying was Steve's dream and the only thing in his life he ever wanted to do. Steve feels a great sense of grief and loss as he grapples with losing something he loves, his dream job. Steve has only ever identified with being a pilot and the lifestyle it affords. He feels angry and lost. Before he can even start to assess other career options, Steve seeks help from a therapist to work through these emotions.

After six months, Steve gets to a place of acceptance about his situation and starts the career exploration process. He can now think more broadly about his skills and strengths. He realizes that his years in the cockpit could be valuable to aircraft simulation manufacturers.

Steve creates a resume for the first time in his career and learns how to sell himself and his skills in a whole new way. Because of his unique experience as a pilot, Steve finds a job as a trainer for an aircraft simulation manufacturing company. What seemed like an impossible career crossroads becomes an opportunity for Steve to spread his wings in a new direction.

THE SUNSET YEARS

Now what? Here is another developmental benchmark where people grapple with career change. They have maximized their earnings, climbed as high as they can go, and now may be on the downhill coast to retirement. Of course, retirement isn't what it used to be. Instead of it being the end of the book, or the career, it is just the next chapter.

Interestingly, at this point in your life there may be the same pressure to choose a direction as you experienced forty years earlier as a young adult. Once again, there are either endless choices or choices limited by financial resources.

 MEET NELL

Back in the day, Nell was at the top of her game, holding the top human resources spot at her company and well respected in her profession and by her peers. When Nell reached sixty years old, she was suddenly downsized, right-sized, and out on the street without a job and without a plan.

She is in earshot of retirement, but believes she can contribute productively for several more years in a professional environment. This is both an exciting and uneasy time. She can't see herself jumping back into a human resources leadership role, much less jumping into the job market. So Nell assesses her life and goals and decides she is going to return to school and get a master's degree in counseling.

Nell currently counsels students at a community college on a ten-month schedule that allows her to spend more free time with grand-kids and at her lake cottage.

Just by the nature of growing up and growing older, career crossroads happen. But it's not the only time.

Crossroads While in the Job

Let's say you have a job, things are clicking along just fine and you are generally content and maybe a bit on autopilot. But one day you wake up and things have changed, seemingly under your feet. This change can be in the nature of your work, in the people you work for, or in the environment and culture around you.

It's been said the one constant in life is change. More than ever, this seems to be the case at work. What is interesting is how long it can take to secure just the right job with all the right elements that match your skills and interests, challenge you, and even provide a pathway for advancement. The job seems perfect in just so many ways. But as time goes by, whether it is little by little or dramatically, the job morphs around you and you no longer get to do the things you enjoy. It is rare that an employer will consult you about any changes in job respon- sibilities; often the changes just happen. You may trust and hope it's for the best; you buckle down and take on the new responsibilities to be a team player. But when the tasks and responsibilities no longer align with your strengths and interests, you might feel restless, anxious, and even disengaged. You are at a crossroads.

 **MEET DAN**

Last year Dan was so happy to land a job as a sales manager, which ended his one-year job search. Dan did his due diligence. The job fit his background, experience, and skills to a tee. However, over the course of the year, his job responsibilities moved from sales management to front line sales and responding to proposals. Dan's strengths fit best in development of top sales teams, but because his job now required so much time on proposals, he couldn't work as effectively with his team.

Dan became increasingly frustrated. He spoke to his boss, but given limited resources, the company needed him as an individual contributor. The job Dan signed on to a year ago has changed.

Dan is at a decision point. He has to evaluate if his new job responsibilities are temporary as the company goes through a rough time or if this is going to be status quo. Dan oscillates between stepping up and showing his versatility, or having a heart-to-heart with his boss. Dan elects to talk to his boss to get a pulse check on what his role will be moving forward. He also sets his own timeline of six months. If he doesn't go back to sales management in six months, he's going to start looking for a new job.

Eight months later, nothing has really changed for Dan so he decides to launch a job search. However, he first has to overcome non-compete issues in his employment contract, not getting a reference from his boss, and the challenge of keeping his search a secret so he doesn't jeopardize his current job.

Dan's search takes over a year and a half. He secures a sales management job for a small company for a lower salary. He resolves that leading people is more important to him than a higher salary, so this career crossroads was worth the change.

Although Dan decided to leave his job and company, other employees may elect to leave a job but stay within a company. This is also a crossroads.

The stepping stones inside of companies are multidirectional. Most people assume that moving only means moving up. But career paths inside organizations are also lateral in which an individual leverages transferable skills in another role.

 **MEET TIM**

Tim has been an engineer for eighteen years. Successful in his role, he craves more people interaction. So Tim speaks to human resources to better understand where in the company they utilize engineers or engineering skills. Tim learns about a technical customer service job that helps customers with trouble shooting issues with the product. Because Tim assisted with design of the product in his former role, this job is a good fit. Tim transfers to that job and works directly with customers every day, maintaining the same rate of pay. He now feels extremely satisfied in his work.

In order to get to a different and better place in your career, you may opt to take less pay for more flexibility or go part-time while reassessing your career options.

MEET CAROL

Carol is a physician in a teaching hospital. Not long ago, she had up to twenty patient contacts a day and made a salary well into six figures. However, Carol started to burn out due to the increased patient load.

Though Carol is well respected in her field as a practitioner and makes a good wage, she realizes through much soul searching that she wants to teach. So Carol steps down as a practitioner and takes a part-time role as a lab instructor at the medical school associated with the hospital at almost a quarter of her previous salary. This allows her to shift from direct patient care into academia, positioning her well to teach a course when the opportunity presents itself.

A few years ago a study by Florida State University bore out what people have said repeatedly. People don't leave their jobs/companies/organizations; they leave their bosses/managers. I often hear people take a job strictly because they like the person who interviewed them. They like their management style, their vision, their ability to mentor, and their leadership abilities. But bosses and managers can change, and sometimes do change, frequently. When the person you rallied behind is suddenly gone, you may also lose your internal ambassador whom you can count on to stick up for you and promote your abilities to others inside the organization. This person may have moved on, moved up, or taken reassignment. Often, without being able to give input, you get a new boss. This new boss may have a completely different style and have different departmental objectives from your previous boss. He or she may come with a team of favorite people. You may struggle to see how you fit into the plans. It can feel like starting over — a crossroads.

MEET MARY

Mary clicked immediately with her future boss during the interview process. It secured her decision to take the job. Two weeks into the job, Mary found out her boss was moving to another division. She was disappointed, but figured things would be fine. The organization wasn't sure if they were going to replace Mary's boss right away. So Mary worked without a boss for three months. All in all it wasn't too bad; she just minded her work. When Mary finally got a new boss from another department, this person didn't really understand Mary's work and wasn't a very good resource or support.

Six months later a new manager is hired and Mary quickly realizes they mesh like oil and water. Their styles are very different, and Mary is never really clear about what is expected from her. Mary likes her job and the company, but interactions with her boss are extremely stressful.

Mary is at a crossroads. She elects to stay in her job and see if this new boss will last. She is committed to making the best of it, but the discord with her boss continues. Four months later Mary fails to complete a performance improvement plan and is terminated.

Choosing a job based on cultural fit can be just as important as the compensation in terms of job satisfaction. So when you find that right cultural fit, there is likely to be a high amount of job satisfaction and fulfillment. But a company's culture can change when the leadership changes or when a merger or acquisition occurs. When this happens, it may feel like your world is changing. The rules have changed, the mission may have changed, and the definition of success may have changed, leaving you uncertain about how to go forward.

MEET JILL

Jill is a finance manager. She works for a company that has a reputation for being employee friendly and an employer of choice in her community. On a daily basis Jill likes her job, feels engaged, and fulfilled. However, this company has recently merged with another company that is a major player within the industry. Given the major organizational and cultural change, Jill no longer sees how her role fits in the big picture; her career path has seemingly dried up.

So Jill decides to explore other jobs that have more of a career path; she launches a quiet job search for similar jobs at other companies within her industry. As part of her search, Jill makes sure to intentionally ask about company culture and internal career opportunities during the job interviews. At this crossroads, she wants to increase the chance of her landing a job at a company whose culture aligns with her value of professional growth and development.

Crossroads on the job are often the most difficult to navigate because at the surface you just feel dissatisfied and discontent. Before being able to make any career decision, it requires the ability to step back and assess what is at the core of that dissatisfaction. Once you can determine whether it is the job, the people, or the culture, you can then evaluate your options.

Crossroads While Between Jobs

Often the most evident and yet tumultuous career crossroads are those between jobs. Whether you intentionally planned the transition or it just happened, the options and path that lie in front of you are often clouded by uncertainty and anxiety.

Even when you purposely decide to leave an existing job, the transition can be still be scary. It takes a lot to harness excitement, fear, doubt, and nervousness, and muster the courage to believe in something better.

The decision to leave a job often starts with a triggering event. These events can be internal or external in nature. External events are situations involving the existing job, the people, or the culture that prompt you to move on.

Internal triggers can include a general restlessness, boredom, or loss of interest or passion. There is also the dreamer factor. You begin daydreaming about a different kind of work life. Whether internal or external, these are all triggers that cause you to start thinking: Is there something else, something better? Now what? In response to these triggers, you go into transition mode.

 **MEET HARRY**

He makes $200,000 a year as a director of marketing, has been doing his current job seemingly effortlessly for seven years — and he is bored. He has lost his zest and is beginning to struggle bringing his "A" game every day. He is disengaged from his work and coworkers and fears that his disingenuousness will start to affect his performance. He knows he has to do something drastic or nothing will change, so he quits his job to take time to re-evaluate himself, his life, and his options. He considers it a professional sabbatical to direct all his energy to evaluating the next step in his career.

Unlike Harry's situation, many job losses are unplanned. When people abruptly lose their jobs through a termination, layoff, or job elimination, they are catapulted into a job transition. They ask, "Now what?" They also ask, "What just happened?" Before clearly evaluating options at this crossroads, you may need to take some time to regroup on an emotional level. When you lose a job, you may go through the same grief stages as you do when anything of significance in your life is lost or ends. It is important you honor this and do the healing work necessary because it is only when you are strong and healthy that you can more clearly see the options that lie before you.

During transition, you can obsessively cycle through the various options in your mind, whether you should jump back into the same kind of role in another organization, or wonder if it is time to do something different. You could take on a dream job or even contemplate working for yourself. All these options swirl around in your mind under a cloak of urgency because being unexpectedly unemployed can feel like a free fall into a black hole, not knowing when the next paycheck will come.

It is easy to imagine doing the same job, just somewhere else. Sometimes you'll choose this path because it seems like the one of least resistance. This is a good time to ask yourself whether you are pursuing this because you can, or because you really want to.

 **MEET JEFF**

After sixteen years as a financial analyst, Jeff's job was eliminated and is in transition for the first time in over ten years. His first instinct is to immediately start scanning the job postings for financial analyst jobs. But when asked why he is looking for those kinds of jobs, he quizzically says, "Because this is what I do." Since he can't say whether that route is a conscious choice for his career or just a default, Jeff agrees to undergo some assessment testing to determine if this career choice still aligns with his life goals and values. Jeff learns his values have changed over the years, and though he still really enjoys the day-to-day work of financial analysis, he wants to do it for an organization that is much more cause and purpose driven.

This finding helps Jeff continue to pursue jobs as a financial analyst, but in the nonprofit sector. This crossroads is a chance for Jeff to align purpose and passion with his career choice.

It takes courage to consider something else or something new, whether it is a traditional 9-5 job or in an entrepreneurial capacity.

 **MEET SUSAN**

Susan's job as a mainframe programmer has been outsourced by her former employer so she is now unemployed. Though it's scary to be without work, Susan recognizes there will be fewer and fewer jobs in mainframe programming in the future. So after meeting with the dislocated workers counselor from the unemployment office, she receives the funding to return to school to learn interactive media—a much more marketable skill right now. Susan currently works for a local newspaper to maximize its website.

MEET SID

Sid was a program manager for eighteen years and lost his job when his company merged with an overseas company. Sid quickly starts to look for program management jobs, but struggles to get excited about anything he finds. The harder he tries to job search, the more he struggles. Finally Sid decides to take a break to reassess his job search and career in general.

During his time away, he realizes that he's burnt out from program management and would really rather go back to something using his hands, which has been a long lost passion of his. Sid is a skilled artist and craftsman, so after taking a self-employment class, he learns he has what it takes to become an entrepreneur. He decides to buy a small picture framing shop. Though his salary is about two-thirds of his previous salary, he is much more passionate about his work and loves going to work every day.

When at a career crossroads while in between jobs, deciding which route to choose has a lot to do with a timeline imposed by financial resources. When you leave or lose a job, the reality of income has an enormous influence on the path you are willing to consider. Understanding your options helps you quickly make a plan and take the next step on your career path, but that assumes you have a clear sense of your direction.

NAVIGATING YOUR
CAREER JOURNEY

So you've reviewed the many ways that people reach a career crossroads and also met people who faced their various crossroads and found new paths. Now, we're going to discuss how to approach the question of "Now what?" The following sections provide you the steps for answering this question for your unique situation. The first step is to get to know yourself again.

Know Yourself

Regardless of what brings you to a crossroads, before you can choose a path and take a step forward, it is actually best to take a step back.

Too often people leap directly from one thing to another without knowing why. Or they passively drift along until fate or circumstance brings them to their next landing. Either way, career moves like these range from passive to impulsive and reactive and are always unplanned.

It is important to take a step back because it allows you to consider things that have changed with yourself, in your life, and in your career. Get clear not only about what you can do, but also commit to what you want to do from this point forward.

At a basic level, assessing yourself includes evaluating your skills, strengths, interests, values, qualities, and motivators.

SKILLS

Skills are things you have learned such as public speaking, working with numbers, or visualizing design. Not everyone shares your skills. Abilities you are both born with can be developed as skills. When assessing skills, realize that you accumulate dozens of skills as you develop professionally. You don't use all of your skills in every single job, so some sit in your tool kit to tap into later. Like any tool, some skills are used for years and some skills become rusty and outdated. When you reach a crossroads, you should sit back, sort through, and intentionally select skills you will continue to use, which skills you may need to sharpen, and which new skills you want to acquire.

Assessing skills can be a difficult task because you often take for granted the things you do with comfort and ease. You assume everyone has that skill. There are four factors to consider while assessing skills at a career crossroads.

- Understand the skills you already possess.

- Determine the skills you want to continue using.

- Figure out how your skills can apply to work.

- Consider new skills (if any) you want to learn to develop.

STRENGTHS

Strengths are like skills. However, they are either highly refined or they are natural talents or gifts. Public speaking is a skill, but it becomes a strength when you excel at it, are recognized for it, or are paid for it. Much has been written about understanding and harnessing strengths. People who use not only their skills, but also leverage their strengths, are the happiest and most successful in jobs.

Assess strengths by looking at your lifelong accomplishments and the things for which others recognize you.

INTERESTS

Interests are the things that engage you, get you jazzed and fulfill you. Interests can be a subject matter, an industry, a cause, or an activity. Too often people keep interests compartmentalized to the weekend and fail to consider how they weave into a career. Interestingly, you accumulate various interests throughout your life, but once examined, you'll discover you gravitate back to the same or similar interests for years. It's often when your interests go unexpressed that you feel something is missing in life.

VALUES

Values are another part of ourselves that factor into career decisions. You might think you have one set of values through life. But your values change based on your developmental stage, age, and life situation. Because of this, values should be reassessed regularly. Think about it: the things that are important to you in your twenties such as first job, first new car, or first apartment are very different from the things you value in your forties like career, family, and health. A career crossroads presents the perfect time for re-assessing your values. These values will then act as an anchor when you evaluate career options.

QUALITIES

One more area to consider at a career crossroads is your qualities. Qualities are characteristics that describe you and sometimes define you. Examples of qualities could be passionate, dedicated, or driven. Others often identify you by your qualities. By understanding your qualities, you can make career choices that play to those qualities.

MOTIVATORS

Finally, knowing what motivates you can help you make smarter career choices. Motivators are what drives you to get up in the morning and what satisfies you. If you choose a job that aligns with your motivators, you will be more engaged in your work.

So how do you assess each of these six factors at a career crossroads? There are dozens of tools and assessments in the market. There are paper and pencil self-assessments you can take through books, magazines, or online. Trained counselors and professionals also provide assessments that include a combination of interviews, tools, and standardized tests.

Remember that assessments are tools that help you better understand yourself. It is the combination of assessments and tools that draws the clearest picture of who you are. The better you know yourself, the better you can approach the various crossroads in your life with confidence. The second step in navigating your career journey is knowing your options.

Know Your Options

Career options are abundant. They really are. For some people, that can be exciting, but the vast majority of people at a crossroads can feel overwhelmed.

You always have options. What you allow as an option comes down to how many trade-offs you're willing to make and your courage to be open to possibility.

Options depend on whether you are currently working, re-entering, or in transition. Are you coming to this decision point with a long work history or with a clean slate? Let's consider options with the following framework in mind.

Career options can be categorized by

- What work you do
- How you do your work (traditional job or as an entrepreneur)
- Where you work (home, organization, company)
- When you do your work (set schedule, flexible).

If you have an established work history, the first point of discernment is if you want to continue doing the same type of work in the same role or function. As addressed in the previous section, skills, strengths, interests, values, qualities, and motivators can help you see how well you align with the job you are doing.

Your first option is to stay in the field or profession you work in. If you enjoy your work, but dislike where you do it because the company or organization may be dysfunctional or a culture that no longer aligns with your values, you may just need to move to another employer within that industry.

When you love the work you do, a second option is to move into a new niche or industry that has the same work. You may elect an industry that is new or growing or is closer to an area you are interested in.

A third option to consider is doing something new. Sometimes that might mean within the same organization. This could include moving into an expanded role with new responsibilities, moving laterally to a different role that both leverages your transferable skills and yet allows you to learn new ones, or moving to a lesser role to gain entry into a whole new career path.

You may want to consider option four, which is starting completely fresh with a new role in a new field or niche. This might require skill enhancement or even retraining.

Remember, there is a difference between the work you do and the nature of how you do it. Contrary to working in a traditional fashion is self-employment. Being an entrepreneur is a career choice; it is the fashion in which people do their work. Self-employment is option five and many people choose it.

For example I am a career counselor. That is my role, function, or profession. How I work as a career counselor can be for an employer or in an entrepreneurial fashion.

Self-employment can take different shapes. It could include buying a business or franchise, starting a business from scratch, or becoming a consultant. Each requires different levels of skill and financial investment.

Though self-employment has its advantages, it is not for everyone. It is very important to take the time to assess if being an entrepreneur is for you.

One type of entrepreneurship is the portfolio career. Portfolio careers consist of two to three different roles done independently of each other in either a traditional or entrepreneurial fashion. Income is generated from each role.

RESEARCH

Research is a large component of understanding your options. The key is knowing what to research, how to obtain the information, and then how to organize it in a fashion that leads to a good career decision.

First let's address what to research. In terms of professions and occupations, you will want to know the technicalities like skills, qualifications, and educational preparation required. You will also want to know what jobs exist within the profession. You will want to know the fields, industries, and organizations where that function or job exists. Research the occupational outlook for a given profession to determine how long a profession will be in demand and the jobs available within that profession.

For example, as a career counselor, my profession is counseling. I could have chosen from many types of counseling like clinical, marriage and family, or drug and alcohol. But I chose career counseling as a specialty. I know it requires a master's degree and skills in the areas of assessment, evaluation, communication, and planning. The fashion in which I practice career counseling is as an entrepreneur in my own practice, though I could have worked in a traditional sense for employers in corporations or in higher education.

How do you obtain the information on your chosen profession? The Internet is a fabulous tool to research occupations, but the best way is by talking to various people in any given profession to truly understand the jobs that exist and what they're like on a day-to-day basis.

Once you do this research, establish a system to capture and organize it in a way so you can quickly and easily see what is required of a great candidate for specific jobs. This is also the time to go back to the assessment work you did about skills, strengths, interests, values, qualities, and motivators to see how they align with each job.

Knowing your options can be both exciting and overwhelming, but when systematically explored, they can lead to a more confident career decision.

After the seemingly exhausting task of sifting, sorting, surveying, and researching all of the options, the most difficult step still lies ahead. It is choosing your destination. This step can be accompanied by the mixed emotions of excitement as well as anxiety and fear, which can bring your career decision to a screeching halt.

On one hand, seeing the end point of all your hard work to navigate through your career crossroad can be very exciting. There is comfort that comes with establishing a goal. It is an end to the dissatisfaction, restlessness, and aimlessness that brought you to this crossroads.

But actually choosing your career path can be the most painstaking. Choosing not only requires clarity of destination, it requires courage and commitment to make it your own. It is about naming and claiming your choice. It is about letting go of all the other options and declaring a choice. What immobilizes people is the fear of making the wrong choice that may lead them down the wrong path. They abandon the confidence in the hard work and due diligence — neglecting to see how making a choice can propel their careers and lives forward.

Being intentional about your choice can be very powerful. It inspires you to continue moving forward on your career path and to take the first step.

Choose to move towards a goal vs. running away from something that is dissatisfying. This is an important mindset to have before moving forward.

Look for alignment with what you now know about yourself and your choice. You will find greater comfort and confidence in your choice when it aligns with who you are at your core. Choosing a destination is equally about the courage to make a choice as much as it is about the actual destination.

Once you've made the choice, a detailed road map will help you reach that destination.

Laying Out a Plan or Roadmap

In the previous section, we covered step two and walked through selecting a career destination and the comfort that comes with committing to it. But, as with any destination, there are many roads to get there, and that's step three — laying out a plan or roadmap to reach your destination.

A roadmap will be necessary to get you there while keeping the destination always in sight. It will outline the steps and stops along the way that are necessary to reach your goal.

When laying out your roadmap, one of the first decisions is how to get to that next point in your career. Will you take the long scenic route? Will you take the shortest route? Will you take a short cut?

Time and resources are the biggest factors in choosing your route — time in terms of age and resources in terms of money. Will you choose the shortest route or a short cut because you need to make a change quickly or believe that advancing age may prohibit a change? Or will money run out so you have to jump on the fast track to your destination? Do you have the luxury of time and money to take the long scenic route?

Set an overall timeline. Do you want to arrive within months or years? For some this process could be as short as a few months and for others it could take years.

First you will want to establish milestones. These are measurable mini-goals to indicate if you are making progress. You can lose momentum in the process, so it is important to know what exactly needs to occur step-by-step to show you are moving towards your goal.

Next is to set an itinerary. This ties your milestones to a timetable so the overall process doesn't seem insurmountable.

Use the know yourself information from step one. The hard self-discovery work you did will act as a compass in the event you hit a detour. Staying true to your core, which consists of skills, strengths, interests, values, qualities, and motivators, is fundamental to the journey.

With the journey outlined and a map in hand, it's time to take your first step in navigating your career crossroads.

Starting the Journey

Whatever circumstance or choice brought you to a crossroads, hopefully you have approached it with grace and a sense of possibility. You looked at yourself and looked at your options. You identified the goal and end point. You are committed to action and moving towards that goal. You've laid out a carefully scripted roadmap. Now start the journey.

It may feel like there is a twenty-five-pound weight attached to your foot right now. Address the various perceived barriers that prevent you from moving forward.

The first barrier is fear. After all the hard work of assessing yourself and your options, will it be the wrong choice? What if you are not fulfilled and happy? You can get caught up in speculations and faulty thinking about worst-case scenarios. Fear can be the biggest immobilizer.

Doubt can also act as a barrier to beginning the journey, doubting the process, doubting your choice, doubting yourself. You either lack the self-confidence to believe you deserve something better or you don't trust in the possibility of finding happiness in work or career choice. You doubt fulfillment in a job can exist.

Both fear and doubt are often anchored in misperceptions and are often self-imposing barriers.

Age can also be a perceived barrier to taking the first step. Sometimes people say they are too old to make a change. They question their ability to venture down a new path, or maybe learn something new. Age is less of a number and more of an attitude and frame of mind. Though age can be a factor, it doesn't have to be a deal breaker.

A self-perceived lack of skills or education can also keep you from moving forward. But good assessment of your core should help in clarifying strengths and transferrable skills, so they are a key consideration when evaluating your options. By this point you should be heading down the road that aligns with your skills and you know exactly what is needed in terms of any skill enhancement, retooling, or retraining. You know your strengths and transferrable skills, so claim them and don't let concern about skill or education be a show stopper at this point.

Another barrier is lack of opportunities. You have to trust in the due diligence you did when assessing your options. Be clear about the potential opportunities that will exist down your chosen path to avoid this barrier.

The following factors will help you overcome these barriers and embark on your journey with confidence.

- Centeredness. Centeredness is an inner peace bestowed by grace and balance in your life and in your heart. When you are centered at your core, you can overcome many barriers.

- Strength. Strength is the energy to pull yourself up from the defeat, despair, or adversity that may have brought you to this crossroads.

- Readiness. Readiness is a sense of timing in your life that allows you to be open to possibility.

- Courage. Courage is believing and trusting in yourself to be able to move beyond your circumstance.

- Commitment. Commitment is making it a priority not to stall at the front or in the middle of the crossroads and to do the hard work necessary to move forward.

- Resources. Resources are the people and things that can help bring clarity and accountability to the process. You will navigate a crossroads much more effectively when you leverage all your resources.

Acknowledging and addressing these factors will help you remove the barriers that prevent you from moving forward and allow you to step into a whole new chapter of life.

Getting Support

Whether it is a toddler hesitantly and tentatively stepping forward, a skydiver who launches himself into the clouds below, or a dancer stepping onto the stage for the first time, not far from their grasp someone is in the background spotting, encouraging, applauding, and supporting along the way. The initial step is not taken alone. It is taken with the support of others. This is also the case along your career path. Every step forward comes with the support of others who play various roles in your journey.

Support may come in the form of family, friends, mentors, or professionals. Each brings a unique perspective and form of support that is equally valuable.

During the career crossroads throughout your life, family is often a consistent force in the background and even in the forefront. Families typically care about us deeply and want us to be happy and successful. In terms of career decisions, they can be helpful as a sounding board and lend insight based on their professional experiences. The best way they can be supportive is to remind you of your great qualities, skills, and strengths.

Friends see you differently than families do. While they also care about you and want you to be happy, friends can provide a different kind of support during career crossroads. They can give great honest feedback about your qualities as well as your flaws that have been patterns throughout your life. They can be great for brainstorming and idea generation. Friends, like family members, are often supportive no matter which road you choose.

Mentors play a unique role in supporting you in career decision-making. They typically know you best as a professional or from your work history. A mentor could be a new person in your life or people who have known you for years. You meet mentors in the classroom, on the playing field, at work, or in the community. They have seen your skills in action. They may have seen your roaring successes or even possibly your painful failures. These are people who you aspire to be and who have taken you under their wings to support, guide, and advise you. They lend a unique objectivity that friends and family cannot. Mentors are wonderful sounding boards, but sometimes give you the unabated advice you are not ready to hear. Mentors are role models. You have seen them walk a path before you and you can learn navigational tips for your own journey.

Unfortunately, not all of us have the great fortune of having a mentor. And sometimes we find it difficult to reach out to family and friends for advice and support.

It is then that reaching out to a career professional makes sense. The types of professionals that can be instrumental in career decision-making can include career counselors, career coaches, and life coaches. These are the most objective within your support network. These are professionals trained in the process of transition. They are skilled in assessment, which helps you gain insight into your skills, strengths, interests, values, qualities, and motivators. They can decipher patterns in your history and help you evaluate options. They are masterful in bringing clarity to your choices and helping identify a clear direction. Professionals will help you establish a plan and milestones to move forward. In addition to support, they can provide an accountability component that helps you make your goals into reality.

The key to getting support is to acknowledge this is not a process to tackle alone. There is an ensemble of people who will help and support you every step of the way, spotting you, encouraging you, and applauding you from the near distance.

CONCLUSION

Various circumstances may have brought you to a crossroads. You will ask, "Now what?" many times through your life and career. We all face these pivotal decisions; it is part of our human experience.

There is no need to struggle or feel isolated upon entering a career crossroads. It is my hope that you have gained a greater understanding and insight as well as gathered the tools to approach a crossroads with confidence and smoothly navigate your way through and come to a place of greater fulfillment in life and in work.

MEET KAREN

She picked a college based on the major she was interested in studying. Career crossroads number one: the major wasn't what she expected and she changed majors to go on an entirely different career path. Career crossroads number two: she had to pick a focus area in graduate school. She landed an assistantship in a different specialty area, and again changed her career path. She landed a great internship and her career was on track until her job was eliminated, resulting in career crossroads number three. She then changed industries. Fast-forward seven years. Despite a great job with a global company, here came career crossroads number four: Karen decided there had to be something more and started her own company.

In twenty-five years, Karen has experienced four major crossroads that caused her to pause at the question: "Now what?" By having a good sense of her core, she navigated these crossroads confidently and knows that as she moves along her career journey for the next two decades, she will be able to approach these times knowing she is not alone.

So as we encounter our next career crossroads and ask ourselves "Now what?", we know we have the tools to navigate the various career paths that lay before us. Everyone deserves a rewarding career, and I wish you all the best in achieving it.

Cultivating Careers helps people realize rewarding careers through planful development, planning, and management. To learn more go to cultivatingcareers.com.

ABOUT THE AUTHOR

 Karen Kodzik is uniquely skilled as a master's level career counselor, as well as an HR and management consultant. As President and Owner of Cultivating Careers, a career management firm, she has helped hundreds of professionals facing difficult career decisions move forward and realize rewarding careers. In addition to her private practice, she is a highly sought after speaker and source to the Twin Cities' media on career management, employment, and job search related topics.

Even as a professional career consultant, Karen, too, has faced the question of "Now What?" in her career. These crossroads led to changing majors, changing cities, changing specialties, changing industries, and starting her own business. The foundation for this book was built on these experiences as well as those of many of her clients.

Karen resides in St. Paul, MN, and can be contacted at Karen@cultivatingcareers.com.